owned by the miners **Tower**

ROGER TILEY

In memory of my grandmother
Gladys Evans (Ann)

photographs by
Roger Tiley

owned by the miners **Tower**

INCLINE
PUBLICATIONS

First published in the United Kingdom by
Incline Publications in 1998

A CIP catalogue record for this book is
available from the British Library

ISBN 0 9522446 1 6

Editorial Angela Tiley
Design Roger Tiley

Book distribution - Incline Publications

With support from The Arts Council of Wales

Incline Publications 1998

e-mail INCLINERT@aol.com

Miners playing in a darts match

For this book I am indebted to an enormous number of people,
for their help and advice - far too many to name. My special
thanks in particular to :

Tyrone O'Sullivan and the management team, allowing me
unlimited access to Tower Colliery to make photographs for this
book.

Tony Jones, Tyrone O'Sullivan and their respective wives for
making me welcome at their homes (thanks for the tea and
biscuits).

Malcolm Howells, Geoff and Hugh, for taking me underground
to make the photographs, and helping to carry my camera equipment.

Rt. Hon. Dr. Kim Howells MP and Rt. Hon. Ann Clwyd MP.
Francis Jones and Liz Manning.

All the miners at Tower, who always welcomed me whilst
visiting the colliery.

Ros Moule for her poetry that has brought this book alive.

Many thanks to Gordon Last, Jake Lior, Paul Seawright, Ian
Walker, Ray Jones and Paul Hurlow for their advice.

Angela, my wife, for her dedication and skill in running Incline
Publications.

My daughter Rhian, and Mam and Dad, for their continued
support; they fuelled my enthusiasm during the production of this
book.

Tower Colliery is situated at the head of the Cynon Valley, north west of Aberdare. It is the last deep coal mine in Wales, carrying on the traditional that once made the South Wales valleys famous. Tower has proved to be a poignant chapter in the history of coal. It is a success story that typifies the strong determination of individuals, widening their knowledge and strengthening their prospects of securing jobs in an area forever seeking to attract new investment.

Tower has witnessed an historic turn-around in its century old story. Owned firstly by entrepreneurs, where greed superseded a commitment to ensure its employees enjoyed an acceptable working and living environment; now the modern entrepreneurs possess morals, with a view to helping their community. The pit is owned by the miners; the share-holders are the workers, who do not want just to profiteer; they want to make an honest living for themselves and reward others; their own people. They want to develop and expand, to create new employment. Their aim is to help and assist towards making their community a better place for future generations.

It is ironic that Tower stands proud, overlooking the surrounding landscape, steeped in history, its people's faces telling the story of pain and struggle. The former owners mansions and mock castles, constructed during the latter part of the past century, are no longer inhabited by the wealthy; the surviving architectural splendour plays home to museums and building which serve the community. Tower takes its symbolic place, not as a monument, but as a coal producer at the forefront of industrial success, which will face the twenty first century with optimism.

From management to manual workers, the aim is to extract coal and find markets in order to secure the future of the pit. The sale of coal, in a highly competitive and diminishing world market determines the life expectancy of Tower. Because of the ever changing demands relating to the sale of coal, predicting the future can be difficult. Miners are confident that the pit can produce coal for the next fifteen years. Indeed, there is plenty of coal to be mined, but the unpredictability of coal extraction and the financial equations of market forces, will inevitably decide the long-term future.

During November 1996, I was invited to make a visual documentation of Tower Colliery. It was unusual to visit a colliery that was not about to close, as I previously witnessed in many other collieries in the South Wales coalfield during the 1980s and early '90s.

On my first visit, I decided to photograph the morning shift coming from the cage and walking towards the pit head baths. I was welcomed with instant friendship and comradeship, which formed the basis of numerous visits during that winter. Unlike any other colliery that I had previously photographed, where understandably, miners wanted to rush to bathe: miners at Tower were willing to stop and be photographed. They even knew how to pose and where to stand for the visiting press photographer. This was the result of constant media attention when the pit re-opened, but not necessarily the images I wanted.

Although I enjoyed every minute of my visits to Tower, the high point of making the photographs for this book was the visits underground. To don the overalls, steel toe-capped boots, helmet and lamp to visit alien surroundings boosts the adrenaline. Reaching pit bottom walking a short distance, and then riding on the conveyor belts, is an experience never to be forgotten. It is technically difficult making photographs underground, because of the dirt, noise and low lighting conditions. But the sheer scale of the underground workings, with roadways stretching for miles to the coalface is worth seeing and was a visual inspiration for me. Although Tower is a highly mechanised modern pit, it felt like I was going back in time.

The story of Tower and its success does not stop at the exit gate to the pit, it reaches far into the community. The miners are proud to recognise the importance of community spirit - the community is proud of the miners at Tower. It was a delight for me to talk to former miners, such as Francis Jones, who started working at Tower Colliery in 1920. To visit the Rt. Hon. Kim Howells MP at his home in Pontypridd and the Rt. Hon. Ann Clwyd MP in the House of Commons.

In a way, when the photographs and text are completed, I feel sad, because my regular visits to Tower to produce the work for this book have come to an end. Though looking at the images, I will always remember the banter and leg-pulling, the fun and enjoyment which I had whilst producing this piece of work. I sincerely hope that Tower Colliery has a long and successful future and will continue to make the South Wales valleys famous for its high quality coal reserves.

Roger Tiley

Rt. Hon. Dr Kim Howells MP at home in Pontypridd

As children growing up in Penywaun in the 1950s and '60s, Tower Colliery loomed large in all our lives. The bus which carried miners up the Aberdare Valley to the pit sometimes had, on the front of it, the curious name "Sinkings" as its destination. Shorthand for Tower Sinkings, it referred to the newest of the shafts which had been sunk after the modernisation of the colliery. My Uncle Byron helped sink that shaft. Like many other kids in the towns and villages which graced our beautiful valley, I had relatives working in Tower.

Later, I had friends who worked there; young men who received superb training as electricians, faceworkers, haulage workers, fitters, shotfirers, engineers and so on. They formed the backbone of a highly skilled and immensely knowledgeable workforce and one, moreover, whose political character reflected an overwhelming desire to create a better and fairer society than the terrible one which their parents had been forced to endure through the inter-war years.

Some of them were promoted through the ranks to become skillful mine managers, like my cousin Brian Williams. Others chose to remain as rank and filers, fiercely proud of the tough, charmed circle to which they belonged. It was this extraordinary collection of men and their families who took the momentous decision, after the closure of this country's collieries in the aftermath of the great strike of 1984/85, to risk their precious redundancy money in a cooperative venture to keep open Tower when mine shafts the length and breadth of Britain were being filled in.

The rest, as they say, is history. Led by a committee of NUM lodge officers and their carefully selected specialist advisers, the operation has gone from strength to strength. Is now the most often-quoted example of a successful cooperative business that I know of and it is fitting that Roger Tiley, a photographer of great experience, should put together this collection of images of the men who have made the Tower project work. I hope that the collection will find its way to every corner of the world, for it will serve I am sure as an inspiration to all of those working men and women who, suddenly, find themselves cast aside as little more than redundant industrial statistics. This collection will remind everyone who reads it that human beings and their communities are the most precious commodities of all.

Dr Kim Howells MP
Parliamentary Under Secretary of State
for Higher Education and Lifelong Learning

Rt Hon Ann Clwyd MP maiden speech to the House of Commons - 7 June 1984

"...My constituency is still very much a mining constituency. There are three pits in the valley, and miners also travel to work at 12 pits outside the valley. Thousands of jobs depend on coal, directly in the pits and in the furnacite smokeless fuel plant. Part of my constituency is bordered by the Brecon Beacons national park, and the spectacular scenery continues along the length of the valley. The great warmth and hospitality of its people was noted even by my Conservative opponent.

However, according to one of the bodies nominated by the Secretary of State for Wales, the Wales tourist board,my constituency does not even exist. In a new tourism report containing a map of the South Wales valleys, the Cynon Valley does not even appear. Instead, the whole area, in which 67,000 people live, appears to have been replaced by a large forest. I realise at one time, before the industrial revolution, a squirrel could jump from tree to tree from the Brecon Beacons to Cardiff. Are we to glean from this omission that the Government intend to continue their savage policy of de-industrialisation? Have they a secret plan to reclaim the Cynon valley and extend the boundaries of the Brecon Beacons national park? If they have, they must think again.

The area is, of course, crippled by unemployment. Almost 19 per cent, or one in five people in the valley, have no work. The area has lost its special development area status, and even the CBI is protesting about the cuts in regional aid. The by-products of the Prime Minister's Victorian values - despoiled landscape and inadequate housing - abound. Half the houses in the valley were built before 1919, and the number without baths is three times the national average. Half the land of the valley still shows the scars left by the old coal owners.

One devastating health statistic in the valley is the rate of deaths from respiratory disease. In England and Wales as a whole, the rate is 50 per thousand, but in the Cynon Valley it is almost 73 per thousand. We need proper compensation for those suffering from emphysema and chronic bronchitis as a result of working in dusty industries. It is a heartbreaking experience - I wish that Conservative Members could share it - to see a miner gasping for breath even while using an oxygen mask. Yet, because he has not been diagnosed as suffering from pneumoconiosis, he does not get a penny in compensation. That is more than wrong, it is cruel and unjust.

Those living in the Cynon Valley today are the inheritors of a strong, radical tradition. One former Member of Parliament, Henry Richard, was known throughout the world as the apostle of peace. Keir Hardie MP, both a pacifist and a socialist, once represented the same area. Aberdare, the main town in the constituency, was one of the two largest and most influential centres of literacy and musical culture in Wales. The output in printing and publishing was prodigious. The brass bands and the choirs, found throughout the valley, today are once again struggling for the future of their existence. They have always provided a cultural back-bone to their communities.

I suppose there must be some nice, concerned and intelligent Conservative Members, but they have not been obvious this afternoon. The point made by my honourable friend was valid. Why is it right to subsidise food surpluses but not right to subsidise coal? But then, one quarter of the Tory candidates in the European elections are farmers. How can we expect any reform of the CAP when the leader of the European Tories is no less a person than Sir Henry Plumb?

Thousands of jobs in the Cynon valley depend on coal, either directly in the pits and the furnacite plants, or indirectly in the engineering workshops and the factories. Hundreds of small businesses are already feeling the loss of miners' custom. But the support given to the miners is unstinted and generous.

The valley will ensure that the miners will not be starved back to work as they were in 1926 - although it must be said that the Government are doing their utmost to do that. Miners and their families are being forced to live off friends, bags of potatoes and the odd £10 off relatives. They are having to cash their insurance policies, raise second mortgages, sell their cars and furniture and live on tick - but the determination to see it through is in no doubt at all.

Miners' wives are not only providing meals for those in need, they are on the picket lines. Those women feel that their communities, lives and families are under attack. The media image of working-class wives whose husbands are on strike has, in the past, been one of urging them back to work and reviling them for not bringing home the pay packets. But the women today are shoulder to shoulder on the picket lines and there is a powerful new image, supportive and as determined as the men.

The miners are seen as fighting for us all. It is a symbolic fight, a fight against two Britain's - the haves and the have nots. It is a protest on behalf of a lost generation of young men and women who have never been able to find a job in the valleys of South Wales. Mining is still a dirty and dangerous industry, but we have been offered no alternative. We are not prepared to be bought off with the offers of fool's gold from Conservative Members this afternoon. The steel workers already rue the day that they took redundancy pay. The miners will not be in the same position.

We need investment in coal, not cuts and closures. South Wales is the only producer of anthracite in Britain. Britain is short of 1 million tonnes of anthracite a year, yet the NCB aim to cut our coking coal pits and refuse to invest in the new mine at Margam, they import into Port Talbot 1 million tonnes a year of foreign coking coal.

Only South Wales and Durham produce those quality coals, yet they are precisely the two areas most discriminated against in new investment in major capital projects. Last year, while the pits of Nottinghamshire and Yorkshire enjoyed new projects under construction to the value of £2.5 billion, South Wales and Durham were scratching along on less than £42 million - less than 2 per cent of the Yorkshire and Nottingham totals. In other words, despite knowledge of massive proven reserves in untapped coalfields such as Margam, the Government are being guided by the same short-sighted advice that caused them to massacre the coal industry in the early 1960s, leaving the United Kingdom to the tender mercies of the international oil companies and OPEC.

The Government are engaged at this very moment in what amounts to nothing less than industrial sabotage. The country needs coal, and we can provide it. The NUM's is not a plea for charity. Closing 74 pits and making 74,000 miners redundant - that is Mr. MacGregor's ultimate plan - would cost £45 billion. To keep them open, producing coal, would cost less than half that, with or without new investment. Success for the miners would preserve their jobs, for the benefit of us all. We want the investment, we want recruitment, we want new technology. There will be no compromise in South Wales."

Ann Clwyd MP
Cynon Valley

Malcolm Howells, surveyor

pit bottom

poem by Ros Moule

A strong man looks forward
Power in his eyes
Hard-won, with his strong team,
He and they, all equal now

Both own and work the mine
True Marxist stance
Within New Labour's state.

He stands in pride of manhood,
god of the ground he moves
bull-shouldered, his crew
and their skilled sinews

making machines do as they will
with keys, grease, cogs, and wheels
to shift the clutter of the cavernous
whale of coal ribs in the dark

that rises like a huge sea dew
to cast on the dawn shore
the trove of coal that gleams
in pristine lorries, substance

of hope for young apprentices
who plant their feet
on the heft and metal
of the best foothold in the world

Tyrone O'Sullivan, Chairman at Tower Colliery

Tyrone O'Sullivan's story

"I was born in Abercwmboi and lived there for many years. You did not see many cars in those days, so as a boy I played with my friends on the road. When it was snowing, you could more or less slide down the road to Mountain Ash and back.

Abercwmboi, before the furnacite plant was built, had three lakes. We used to go swimming, not only in the Summer, but all year round. When I think back to those days, it always seems like Summer and my memories are of us playing, although we did go to school. Our village, like many others in the valleys was self-contained. The local grocers provided our food, although there wasn't the choice of food that there is today in supermarkets. Our clothes were bought locally along with odds and ends for the house. Whilst the men were at work in the local pit, the women would do their shopping. The village was bustling in those days. In the Summer, most families in our street would sit on the wall outside their homes and entertain themselves by indulging in local gossip. As a boy, the Summer seemed to be a lot hotter and our parents sat on cushions because the wall used to get so hot it would burn your back-side. Everybody's door was open, nobody would pinch other people's possessions otherwise they would not be welcome in the community. The miners were hard and they would not put up with any nonsense.

My father was a miner, and from the day I was born, coal mining was in my blood. I started in the pit at the age of fifteen, training at Aberaman Colliery in 1961. I remember the first day walking up the pit with my father. Everybody would do their training at Aberaman: boys came from the Rhondda, Cynon Valley and Merthyr. It was the teddy-boy era; a tough time in those days, as gangs of boys from different villages would be in conflict.

When I finished at Aberaman Colliery Training Centre I went to Fforchaman Colliery to train underground. I found that incredible; from leaving school where the environment was clean, to working in a coal seam which was two feet three inches in height. By the time you put your duffel-bag down, you had about eighteen inches of room to work in. I was as thin as a rake at the time and every bone in my body was aching. I worked, came home, had my dinner and slept until the next morning. My life entailed sleeping and working, but the comradeship amongst the miners underground was terrific. You grew up from a boy to a man, mentally and physically in a matter of a week. Your body became muscular because most of the work was carried out using sheer muscle. One of the work men I was working with then, was Will Chivers. He had enormous arms and shoulders, and legs like bean-poles. The face workers extracted coal lying on their backs, or kneeling if they were lucky. Their upper-body strength was incredible.

After my training, I passed my exam and started in the college at Aberdare as an apprentice electrician. I worked in Abergorki Colliery in Mountain Ash until I became qualified as an electrician. In 1967, Abergorki Colliery closed and I went to Tower to work.

My father was killed in Tower in 1963. I remember a man coming to tell me whilst I was studying at Aberdare College, that my father had been killed. Coming home that day was the worst day of my life; my house was full of people crying. My mother and younger brother and sister were very upset. He was not only a good father, but one who took a major role within our family and he was respected and liked within our community. He was killed when the roof in the district he was working in collapsed. He was trapped when the roof came down on him, but still alive. While the rescuers discussed the best way to get him out, there was a second fall: he died of suffocation. When my father's body was brought to the house, bar a few cuts to his face, he was unscarred. It is ironic that I ended up working in the same pit where my father died, although not in the same underground workings. The district that my father was killed in closed the day after his death and was never worked again. A year before my father's death, nine men were killed in an underground explosion at Tower. Mining is a dangerous profession: we can see that if we look through the history books. With modern mining techniques though, it is a lot safer and Tower Colliery prides itself on safety at work.

As well as the image of hard, uncompromising miners we have the reputation of sticking together. We are proud of the history of our union and of course the South Wales coalfield was the strongest area within the National Union of Mineworkers. I became involved with the National Union of Mineworkers from the beginning of my career in the pit. I was a youth representative in Abergorki: that was a big lodge, it included the Deep Duffryn surface area. A rule was passed allowing youth representatives to sit on branch committees. The requirement to sit on the youth committee was to be under twenty one years of age. This was later moved to under twenty three, as nobody was young enough starting work in the industry.

When I went to Tower, I became a member of the union lodge in 1969, just before the surface-men's strike, when seven pits in Wales and ten pits in Yorkshire went out on strike against the wish of the National Executive. We won the fight and the working hours of the surface-men were reduced. As a trade-unionist, I started my career with a victory. I was hooked, because I had a say in working conditions for the men.

In 1971, I was elected Compensation Secretary and in 1972 Assistant Branch Secretary. A year later, I became N.U.M. Branch Secretary of Tower until 1995, when the pit was bought by the miners.

During the 1984/85 Miners' Strike, I was chairman of the Cynon Valley Strike Committee. There were no 'scabs' at Tower, except for one man who went into work the last day of the strike. He went in at 9.00 a.m. and came out at 10.00 a.m. He wasn't actually a Tower miner; he was transferred during the strike. It is said that as result of the miners' strike, more pits were closed. I have no doubt whatsoever, if it was not for the strike, pits would have closed immediately. The strike sustained the position for a number of years in pits in the South Wales coalfield.

The Cynon Valley Strike Committee was very active during the Miners' Strike. I would be inclined to say that Tower Colliery had more pickets out on duty than any other pit in Britain. We always filled three buses travelling to various picket lines everyday during the strike. We travelled all over Britain to speak at rallies and gain support. Although we spent a lot of our time trying to stop 'scabs' going into work in the Nottingham coalfield, because we were not allowed to get anywhere near the bus convoys, we realised our tactics had to change. Because the miners and their families were facing severe hardship, we began to gain support from many areas in Great Britain and indeed abroad. Amongst the areas that helped towards the strike-fund was support groups founded in Islington, London and Poole in Dorset.

Although less than five percent of miners went back to work in South Wales during the strike, much of our time during the latter six months was spent on picket lines in the valleys. We were also trying to stop the convoys going into the steel works.

When the strike ended, we voted not to go back to work, because the Coal Board would not agree to reinstate the miners that had been sacked during the strike. Between three and four hundred men had been sacked in South Wales alone. The N.U.M. made an agreement with British Coal, so that sacked miners could return to work. The South Wales miners were leading an amicable return to work, although we had the least 'scabs'. I did not agree to the return without our sacked comrades.

After the strike, I felt that there was a split in the N.U.M. in South Wales. We were known as a militant area, traditionally left of centre within the union. Now, the area disagreed with many of the arguments put forward by Arthur Scargill, the President of the National Union of Mineworkers. Although the Government felt that they had defeated the miners, the South Wales miners returned to work and had gained respect and sustained their solidarity. The Government might have defeated the N.U.M. leadership, but they had not defeated the rank and file. After the strike, I felt that the pit closure programme was accelerated because the Government feared the 180,000 miners that were left. They realised that the miners are not led from the top, but from the miners themselves. So, if there were no pits, there would be no miners and no union. Arthur Scargill was just a symbol of the union - he was not the National Union of Mineworkers.

Many pits in South Wales closed purely for political reasons. I have no doubt, the cheapest way to make electricity is by means of coal - it always has been. Other forms of energy including oil and nuclear power have never been cheaper than coal. Europe is one of the few areas not investing in their coal industry. I am convinced that there should be between seventy and eighty pits still producing coal in Britain: they could be producing economic coal. Even after the turn of the century, coal will be a major contributor to our energy needs. Whether a future government will re-invest in expanding our coal industry, remains to be seen. A brand new pit would cost between thirty to forty million pounds. If Britain once again became a major coal producing area, it would have to be a government strategy.

The future of Tower is good. There is plenty of coal to be mined in the area - we will never run out of coal because there are no colliery boundaries now: there is no other deep mine in South Wales. Whether or not we can bring coal to the surface economically is another matter. I cannot see us running out of, what I call, economic coal for at least fifteen years, providing the price per tonne is roughly the same as it is today, taking into account inflation rates.

In South Wales, we could possibly witness the sinking of new coal mines using the drift method rather than sinking deep mines. The size of coal mining would never be on a scale of the old days: that has gone forever. Many of the pit closures after the Miners' Strike up until 1993 can only be blamed on a Tory Government, intent on closing pits for political reasons. But the Tories did not want to close Tower yet, as it was making a large profit and therefore a jewel in the crown, ready for privatisation of the coal industry.

In 1993, local management working for British Coal could see the profits being made in other private industries such as gas, steel and tele-communications. Buy-out bids made millions of pounds for individuals over-night. When local area managers decided to recommend closure of Tower, after the industry was privatized, they would make a bid to buy the colliery. Meetings were being held away from the pit regarding new wage structures, extended shifts and reduced holidays, but the union lodge was aware of this. I knew that if the management wanted to buy the pit, they would have to close it quietly with minimum media coverage. Other pits closed with a few days of media attention and then were never heard of again. Even Maerdy Colliery, the last pit in the Rhondda closed with little opposition. Tower N.U.M. was informed the pit was closing because of geological problems and there was no market for our coal. The Tower union lodge decided to fight the closure and not accept the £9,000 tax-free pay-out on top of our redundancy payment. Miners in other pits always ended their fight for their pit, afraid that they would lose the additional payment offered with a short deadline.

Ann Clwyd, Member of Parliament for Cynon Valley, stayed underground in order to gain publicity. The fight to keep our pit open became an international issue. We had already gained extensive publicity during the previous year, being the last deep mine in South Wales. When Tower closed, we had a fourteen day period to fight the closure and we made it impossible for management to buy the pit, as they were the ones that said the pit had major geological problems and there was not a market for our coal. We forced them into telling the media that there was no future for the pit.

Within ten days of the pit closing, we put our own bid together to buy the pit. Tower was the last pit to close under British Coal in South Wales: I believe we earned that. Throughout our history, we have had a strong union lodge that has the ability to organise, and the strength to fight against destruction. The Tories were afraid to close us, because they knew we would fight until we had won. Even John Redwood, the then Secretary of State, respected our militancy.

When we put forward a bid to buy the pit, we held a meeting to see how many miners were interested in becoming a share-holder and employee of Tower. 174 men came to the meeting and were asked to give an initial amount of £2,000 each. Within four days, each miner had paid the amount. Eventually we built up to 239 men who were interested in joining us. Each miner then gave a further £6,000 and every employee would have an equal amount of shares. Everybody that joined were not sure that they had a job to go back to. But when we obtained the pit we were still not sure if we could sell the coal. In the event, Tower Colliery sold four hundred thousand tonnes, so we were recruiting up until the last minute. The pit had such a successful start, that we recruited trainees who were sons of miners.

At present, there are three hundred employees working at Tower. In addition, there are fifty contractors working underground and forty on the tip; they are not share-holders.

My job in the new Tower Colliery as chairman, is similar to my job as Branch Secretary in the old Tower Colliery. I want to get the best working conditions and wages for the men as possible. I want them kept in employment and protected from unlawful sacking. If I think management are wrong, or even the men, I will tell them. My role is more influential in the company now. Miners have always been proud to see quality anthracite come from their pit and I think management should treat them with respect. We all work together now: its not them and us anymore; it's us all now.

In a modern coal mining environment, we use the same methods as British Coal used, but we are more organised. The miners know their jobs inside-out. The management team listen to the men if they feel working methods can be improved. Absenteeism is low: last year it was only 0.3 percent. The men are multi-skilled now, not only underground but on the surface as well. Employees are flexible, covering a number of different jobs. Take the pit head baths: there are seven men working there. Now, for example, the lampman can cover the medical centre and so on. The company has recognised multi-skill jobs with a reward of increased rest days for share holders. The company wants to recognise the shareholders' versatility in their respective jobs and positively strive to offer benefits: we don't want to cut jobs. Although Tower is still a male-dominated environment, perhaps women will be attracted to mining in the future. Since 1986, the law states that women could work underground in this country. There is no job a woman could not do underground in our day and age. Of course, it's a man's environment; there are no toilets and the language used is an education for people outside the industry, but I am sure the modern woman would get used to that: we are equal after all.

Tower Colliery believes in helping the local community and sponsor many sporting and cultural activities in the area. There isn't a rugby or football team in the valley that has not received money from us. We donate money to cancer research, the disabled riding school, the annual carnival, local athletics, the Cwmaman Brass Band and many other charities.

Tower is the second highest male employer in the Cynon Valley. I've got faith in the future of the Cynon Valley. With new road links, I think more industry will be attracted, providing jobs for our younger generation. Tower Colliery is a success and I am proud to be able to contribute to employment in the Cynon Valley."

Tyrone showing dignitaries around the
visitors centre at the pit

Rt. Hon. Ann Clwyd MP, Member of Parliament for the Cynon Valley.

Houses of Parliament, London

Rt. Hon. Ann Clwyd MP's story

"I actually come from Denbigh in North Wales, but we lived in Halkyn, Flintshire until I was 14. It was an industrial area where lead was mined; I remember the waste tips, on the mountains above the village. When you grow up in the middle of a heavily industrialised area, you do not see the ugliness of it. It was very much like the coal mining areas in South Wales.

At the age of 21, after leaving university, I started work as a reporter for BBC Wales Television in Cardiff. One of the first programmes I worked on featured the valleys. This was my first visit to the South Wales valleys, although as a child, our family had relatives in the valleys and every Christmas we received presents from them; we affectionately called them 'Auntie South'.

I became interested in coal mining when I experienced the ill health and suffering that miners and their families witnessed in the 1960s. With my involvement in the National Union of Mineworkers, I helped to campaign in order to secure better compensation for miners with dust related diseases.

The first time I went underground was in 1974, when I was writing an article for the Guardian newspaper. Having to crawl to the coal face was a frightening experience and I remember thinking that Ted Heath, then Prime Minister, and his Conservative colleagues should be made to come and witness the treacherous conditions miners worked in.

In 1979, I was elected to the European Parliament and in 1984, I fought a by-election, and successfully won the Cynon Valley seat. My first nomination for the seat was from the late Bill Parfit, who was an N.U.M. Lodge Secretary at the time. I remember walking into his house and meeting him for the first time. He had already completed my nomination form and passed it over the table to me saying, 'I was expecting you to call'.

During the campaign, in May 1984, there was a heat wave. Many of the people were sat outside their houses: it was a good time to go canvassing. The year-long miners' strike was on at the time. I remember seeing hardship in the Cynon Valley - families could not afford to eat proper meals, or pay their mortgages. Many families are still in debt to this day. Seeing the despair on children's faces told a depressing story. I invited a Tory MP to visit the Cynon Valley with me; even he was shocked over what he had witnessed. I remember him saying, the Conservative Party was never about bringing suffering and despair on people like this.

In a way, the miners' strike was an exhilarating and busy time. I was involved in meetings that organised the introduction of soup kitchens and the distribution of food parcels in the area. The women in the valleys were fantastic during the strike: many of the miners' wives spoke in public meetings and rallies. They became a strong force in their own right. It was a period in time for great community effort.

The subsequent closure of so many pits had a devastating affect on the South Wales valleys. The last deep pit that survived was Tower Colliery, in my constituency. When the announcement was made to close the pit, it was unbelievable. Tower was profitable and productivity had constantly improved. I think that Margaret Thatcher's particular vindictiveness towards the miners was apparent, and Michael Heseltine, then the Minister for Trade and Industry, was un-sympathetic to the coal miners of Great Britain. I did everything I could, as a Member of Parliament and more, to fight for Tower Colliery and its survival. One evening, I was speaking to Tyrone O'Sullivan, the then Lodge Secretary of Tower Colliery. I asked him if there was anything else I could do to help save the pit from its unjust closure. We talked about a possibility of a protest in the form of a 'sit-in', underground.

I left London on the morning of 14 April, travelling to South Wales not knowing if the underground protest would take place. On arrival in Aberdare, I was told that the 'sit-in' was on: my secretary stuffed some Mars chocolate bars into the pocket of my coat. I travelled up to near-by Hirwaun and was transferred to a van where Glyn Roberts and I, sat in the back. I remember getting out of the van at the drift entrance, where one man was on duty. We pretended to pose for photographs, and when he turned his back, we quickly disappeared into the pit via the drift entrance. It was very slippery and dark, and the draft flowing through the drift was so powerful, it prevented us from walking slowly: it pushed us down to the bottom. By now, the worker at the drift entrance had notified the management who greeted us at the bottom of the descent into the pit. He ordered us to go back, but we refused. Ironically, not knowing at the time, I was wearing a helmet and a belt containing a lamp and emergency respirator, which belonged to the Manager.

We were not allowed to go any further into the pit, so we stayed where we were. It was very cold, but well lit. There were members of the management team regularly guarding us during our stay which lasted twenty seven hours. Although I don't like Mars bars, the ones in my coat pocket became very appetising. Glyn and I sat on a trunk containing first aid equipment. There was also a blanket inside, but we were told not to use this. The members of management who guarded us treated us badly: if they had treated us better, they would have had more positive publicity from the media covering the Tower story.

As the day turned to night, we were cold and very uncomfortable. To try and get warm, we curled up on the floor near one of the vents. There was dust blowing around, which was not healthy for our lungs. We were periodically being woken-up by the management team, who were sharing shift duties, to make it as uncomfortable as possible for us. They used the excuse, that miners underground were not allowed to sleep. During the night, I was told that a woman had come down through the drift to bring us food and blankets. I wrote a note, which was passed to her via a manager, explaining for her to return to the surface, as it was dangerous underground. We never received the food and blankets that she had brought for us.

After twenty seven hours, a member of the N.U.M. passed a message to us stating that the plans for the pit to close had been reversed. I felt this was hard to believe, and remember thinking to myself that it can not be as easy as this to reverse British Coal's decision. But we were assured that the news was true and we walked to the pit bottom, escorted by management, ready to ascend up the shaft the official way, via the cage. When we got to the surface, the press, television and our friends were waiting to greet us.

We felt that we had won a battle against the Tory Government; but most of all, won a battle for the people of the Cynon Valley. Though it is sad to think that so many pits have closed in the valleys when there is a market for fossil fuels, Glyn and I had helped to secure jobs and to keep the pit open.

When the Tower miners decided to form a worker's cooperative to buy the pit, Michael Heseltine sent some of his ministers to the tea room of the House of Commons to discuss the future of Tower. The message was clear, they asked me to tell the miners to throw-in the towel. But John Redwood, the then Secretary of State for Wales, pledged his support to the Tower miners' buy-out."

Francis Jones, a retired miner who spent most of his life working at Tower

Francis Jones's story

"I started work as a collier's boy in the old Tower Colliery number one, on 15 February 1920, on my sixteenth birthday. I worked underground in the district we used to call 'the old four feet seam'. There was two drift mines in those days; I worked in the one which was opened in 1897; both drifts worked the same coal seam. In March 1921 they closed the district I was working in, laying me off for a short period of time. This was the only break in my forty nine year service working at Tower. If my memory serves me right, there was a strike in April of 1921.

In 1919, Tower was taken over by D.R. Llewellyn, previously being owned by the Bute Company. In those days I was a member of the Miners' Federation Union. We were paid for the amount of coal that was mined. The collier's employed 'check wires' to check the weight of the coal trams. They made sure that the collier was paid the correct wage for the coal he mined.

In 1926, the mine owners were refusing to recognise the Miners' Federation Union. It was similar to the 1984/85 coal strike, when the Nott's miners rebelled and formed their own union. Men came from England to work in the pits in 1926; they were the Spencer Union men. We called them 'the white guards'.

During the thirties, up to about 1934, the mine owners had difficulties in selling coal. I walked up to the pit to find there was no work, so the union lodge arranged with the owners, that the miners would work for three days. We worked three days at the end of one week, and three days at the beginning of the next. This enabled us to claim dole for the rest of the week.

Powell Duffryn bought the pit in the mid-thirties and the sale of coal increased. I always remember going to Cardiff to watch the rugby international. The rail sidings in Cardiff were full of wagons carrying coal, waiting to be exported. In my mind, Powell Duffryn were good employers: the manager was George Watson. With the owners, he changed the method of working. There was a fixed wage for filling trams of coal. They paid us for the output of coal, when previously, we were only paid for large coal, and not the scraps. All the best seams by now, had been worked. But the introduction of a cutter enabled us to work smaller seams more efficiently. Previously, we worked with only a pick and shovel. Of course, there was no conveyors to take the coal to the surface, as there is today.

I became secretary of the Tower union lodge in June 1938. During that time the union collected 6d every week from each miner: the lodge was at the bottom of Tower Road. We were not allowed to collect union funds from the miners on colliery property.

The introduction of cap lamps was a major benefit for the colliers. We still had to have an oil lamp in each district. I remember an inspector coming to the pit and finding miners only using camp lamps on an open face. The regulations clearly stated that oil lamps should be present in each district and one in eight men should carry an oil lamp. Although safety was becoming very important, there was not enough oil lamps in the lamproom to go around. We went on strike for a week and after that there was plenty of oil lamps.

I finished in the pit during February 1969. I was awarded the British Empire Medal for my service in the coal industry. Coal mining has come a long way since my day. I was reading in the paper about a new shearer Tower had purchased. They are travelling over three miles to the face now. In the old days, you were not allowed to cross another colliery's boundary. I think the boys at Tower have done a marvellous job, keeping the pit open and keeping men in work."

Tony Jones with his wife, at home in Penrhiwceiber

Tony Jones's story

"In 1961, I left school at the age of fifteen to start work in the pit. After spending a three month period at the National Coal Board training centre, I went to work at Penrhiwceiber Colliery. I worked in the 'Ceiber' until it closed in 1985. My first job in the pit was a measuring clerk: I used to measure the areas on the coal face for the miners to cut the coal. In those days, we did not have power loaders, all the work was carried out by power pick and a shovel. When the power loading method of coal extraction took over from more traditional methods, measuring clerks were no longer needed.

I was offered two jobs at the pit: the one was to work in the surveyors department and the other to work on the coal face; that was the job I took. After five years I became assistant dust control officer. I had to learn the ropes from a bloke who was due to finish later that year, and I would then take over his position. The dust control officer is responsible for good working practices regarding dust underground. I check all the mine workings, making sure the dust levels are low. Modern mining methods have eliminated much of the dust problems, with the cutters on the face using water sprinkler systems which are regularly checked. Years ago, dust related health diseases were common with miners working underground, although dust has not disappeared and is still a problem underground today. We use calcium chloride to keep dust levels down on the floor through the underground workings which run for miles. As part of my job, I am also responsible for checking fire hydrant and extinguisher equipment. The pit is still a very dangerous place, so if there was an emergency, all the safety equipment must be in full working order.

Before Penrhiwceiber Colliery closed, there was talk of the pit being linked underground with Deep Navigation in Treharris. Tower was linked with Maerdy, but Maerdy Colliery in the Rhondda Fach closed soon after the merger. If 'Ceiber' and Deep Navigation had linked together, our pit might have been able to stay open for a few years longer; but who knows! When the announcement was made for the 'Ceiber' to close, we were all devastated. I had been there all my working life and, even as a kid, the pit was always the focal point of the village. Nobody could predict the future of the village, as the pit was the largest employer which paid good wages and therefore much of the miner's money was spent in local shops and pubs. The 'Ceiber' had a reputation of being a militant pit, but realistically, we could not do anything to save the colliery. After the hardships of the year-long miners' strike of 1984/85, we were all trying to get back on our feet from debts and hardship and the news of the pit closing was the final nail in the coffin: I felt so upset.

The last six months at the pit was terrible: there was no atmosphere anymore. The boys were always laughing going down the pit before, but we were like zombies until the pit closed. I will never forget when the 'Ceiber' was being demolished, it hurt me so much. We were all unsure about our futures; some took the redundancy payment, but about fifty of us decided to transfer to Tower Colliery at the top of the Cynon Valley. We all thought that Tower would close in a few years, but at least I would have a few extra years working. With doubts like that in your mind though, I've had a few sleepless nights. Looking back, I made the best move transferring to Tower.

My wife and I are happy living in Penrhiwceiber: we've got a nice house; its not a palace, but we like it here. Our children have grown up: my son went to university and has a good job and my daughter runs a hairdressing business: they both live in the Cynon Valley. I never wanted my son to go down the pit because of the dangerous nature of coal mining, but I would personally never want to work anywhere else. My hobbies include watching the local football team and having a couple of pints with the boys. We are a proud hard working family."

Liz Manning and her son, Aberdare

Liz Manning's story

"My father started working in the pit when he left school at the age of thirteen. He worked in Brown's pit near Cwmaman and ended his working life at Tower Colliery.

The memory I have as a child, is of my father having a hard job. He literally went from bed to work and back to bed again, with meals in between. Dad was on nights regular and was unable to find time to socialise in the week because of his job.

In the 1950s, Aberdare was known as the 'queen of the valleys'. The Italian cafes were the focal point of village culture, along with the chapels and pubs. The chapel for the boys in the pit, was the miners' welfare hall. Saturday was a special day for families, especially the women. People dressed up to shop in Aberdare town centre. There was two cinemas, which were always full.

As a child in the fifties, our play ground was the coal tips. I remember crawling under a fence with my friends in a nearby pit, to play in the coal trams. Our parents allowed us out to play and they never worried about us being abducted, unlike today; you cannot let the kids out of your sight.

Although the Cynon Valley was covered with coal tips on the hillside, I remember the hills being covered in carpets of bluebell flowers. The views across the valley were gorgeous. We played on the 'wimberry' fields, well known in Cwmaman. By the 1960s, they started building factories on green field sites - factories that employed men and women. This was new in the valleys, because women in the past generally stayed at home with the exception of professional women such as teachers and nurses. But the sixties was a time when many families felt unsettled. I remember my father talking about pits being ear-marked for closure. Our family was not scared, as the miners from one pit could be transferred to another, but miners transferring were anxious in the knowledge that they would be moving to a new pit. Although we think of miners as strong macho men, they had their 'butties' in the pit and they did not want to be separated from them. Being transferred was like being moved to another country.

The miners were proud: they gave their wives the house-keeping money each week and allowed themselves the remainder for beer money. Some miners were religious and never went into the pubs or clubs in the village. But underground, the comradeship was incredible. They looked after each other; many of course were related - father and son, brothers and brothers in law. Families were close; it was common to buy a house in the same street as your parents.

When the local pit closed, my father went over to the Maerdy pit in the adjacent Rhondda Valley to work. He always said about the fantastic view that he saw coming over the mountain after the night shift. The sun rising through the mist as he passed over the Rhondda Fach, was a beautiful sight, and it was even better after working underground for so many hours. But miners started to move from pit to pit on a fairly regular basis. Even in the sixties, the communities started to become disjointed, but alternative work was available locally then. In our day of course, it is very difficult to find employment in your local village. Men and women are prepared to travel to places as far as Cardiff and Swansea for work.

After working in a factory for six months, my father came home one Friday afternoon and said to my mam that he was not going back to work on Monday. He obtained a job at Abergorki Colliery, but ended his mining career at Tower. He was caught in a rock fall underground and was badly injured. His arm was smashed and he had serious facial injuries, but he eventually went back to work, and on the first day, after walking a mile from the pit bottom, he suffered a heart attack. After that, he was not allowed to return to work and he later died at the age of fifty four."

The closure of Tower Colliery by Rt. Hon. Ann Clwyd M.P.

22 March 1994
Ann Clwyd tables the following Early Day Motion (EDM) in the House of Commons.

"This House deplores the pressure that British Coal and the Government are putting on the remaining 400 miners at Tower Colliery in the Cynon Valley, the last pit in South Wales, to leave the industry before the enhanced redundancy scheme expires on 30th April; and calls on British Coal and the Government to extend the scheme up to privatisation, so that miners in pits now working can leave the industry with dignity or retain their jobs with the new owner."

31 March
Tower miners arrive at the Department of Trade and Industry, following a week long march for jobs. Ann Clwyd and Dennis Skinner meet them on arrival. The President of Board of Trade, Michael Heseltine, who is in the building, refuses to meet the miners. They hold a meeting in the street instead. Officials of the DTI gives thumbs up sign from upstairs window! Ann takes them to the House of Commons for a drink.

5 April
British Coal issue a press release expressing *'serious concern about the future viability'* of Tower Colliery.

6 April
British Coal issue a second press release to announce the closure of Tower by 15th April.

7 April
Development work at Tower is halted.

9 April
Tower NUM members vote by 92 votes to 70 to put the mine into the modified colliery review procedure. thereby rejecting immediate closure, and a £9,000 sweetener. The review could run for 4-7 months. It is the first time a local workforce has ever refused extra redundancy to fight for their pit instead. British Coal question the result of the ballot.

11 April
Stories of widespread intimidation of miners by British Coal begin to emerge.

12 April
Having withdrawn the offer of £9000, British coal offer it again, if they hold a secret ballot by 14th April. British Coal also state that the new redundancy scheme will be much worse than the existing one.

13 April
Ann Clwyd tables another EDM:

"This house condemns British Coal's announcement that Tower Colliery, the last pit in South Wales and one of the 19 core pits designated in the Government White paper last year, is to close; recognises that the total loss of 400 jobs in the Cynon Valley, where one in five are already unemployed, will result in a further £10 million being lost to the local economy; notes that Tower has made a profit of £28 million in the last three years and had a productivity rate of twice the national average in 1992; and calls on British Coal to accept that decision in good grace and refrain from putting future pressure on individual miners to ignore it."

13 April
Unions are told that if the pit is still in the review procedure by Saturday, British Coal will withdraw it, restart it with new production targets, the present redundancy package will be withdrawn after 30th April and grades and rates will go back to basic. The miners are given until midnight on Friday to decide. The NUM ask for the statement, targets and each man's implied wage cut to be put in writing.

BBC Cefax carries the following page:
"British Coal has said it is ready to withdraw its plans to shut Tower Colliery - the last deep mine in South Wales. A spokesman said if unions remained opposed to the closure on Friday it would drop the proposal and the pit would continue in production. **He denied that the withdrawal was linked to pay cuts and new targets. Unions had said the 250 miners had been told they would have to accept a pay cut to keep the pit open.**"

Ann Clwyd speaks to Neil Clarke, Chairman of British Coal. She tells him that British Coal are making up the rules as they go along - as though there is some political agenda driving them towards closing Tower at all costs. Ann arranges a meeting with Clarke, to take place on 19th April.

14 April
Manager refuses to give union written confirmation of new coal targets.

Meanwhile, after overnight planning, Ann Clwyd enters Tower Colliery, saying *"I intend to remain underground as long as the miners here feel my presence is helpful and until Neil Clarke, the Chairman of British Coal, puts the colliery into the Modified Review Procedure."*

In the local NUM's words,
"all hell broke loose in pit. Management furious."

15 April
Denial of food and drink to Ann by British Coal is raised in the House by Max Madden and Dennis Skinner. The speaker, Betty Boothroyd, replies, *"I hope that her welfare is not neglected by the Coal Board, and I hope that my words will have been noted by the Coal Board this morning."*

Later, Brian Sedgemore raises British Coal's refusal to allow Ann Clwyd to speak to her secretary on the telephone to deal with constituency business.

At the morning meeting, Tower NUM vote by 80% to uphold the decision taken the previous Saturday. **Proposal to close Tower withdrawn by British Coal** *"in the light of the strength of the NUM's feeling and the union's optimism for the future of the colliery"*. (Further to quotes re: pay and conditions from press release) Ann Clwyd emerges after 27 hours underground.

EDM tabled by Michael Clapham and others:

"This House supports the honourable Member for Cynon Valley in her initiative on 14th April of going underground to meet miners at the threatened Tower Colliery; and calls on British Coal to put the closure proposal into the modified colliery review procedure and to ensure that the wages of the mineworkers are maintained at their present level for the duration of the procedure."

It is agreed that Arthur Scargill will address the miners on 18th April.

18 April

Miners at Tower arrive for work. A list comprising of every miner at Tower, with a new, lower rate of pay for each of them, is given to NUM lodge secretary. The lodge decides to call a further meeting to explain to the men that they no longer have the protection of the review procedure and at some time in the near future could be pulled out.

Also on 18th April, Ann Clwyd speaks to Neil Clarke, Chairman of British Coal.

Clarke tells Ann a completely different story to that being told by local management in Wales.

Ann also discusses situation with Arthur Scargill and with employment lawyers.

19 April

Tower miners told that they have until 6.30pm to decide whether, in the light of the new information regarding pay and redundancy terms, they wish to continue to keep the pit open. George Rees, Secretary of the South Wales NUM, is refused a twenty four hour extension to this deadline. Ann Clwyd spends all morning on the phone to: lodge officials; and eventually pins down Neil Clarke, who denies that pay is being cut or that there is a deadline.

During Question Time, Ann attacks the Government's pit closure programme, which has *"dumped thousands of former miners on the economic scrap heap, like the miners at Tower Colliery, who this afternoon were forced to accept closure because yesterday the wages of every miner at the pit were cut.*

"British Coal and the Secretary of State have lied through their teeth."

When asked by the speaker to rephrase her last sentence, Ann first refers to "blatant untruths" and then to the "peddling" of untruths, a phrase used by the Prime Minister the previous week. Outside the House, Ann accuses British Coal of conducting "psychological warfare" on the miners.

Ann cancels a pre-arranged meeting with Neil Clarke, since there is no longer any point in going ahead.

22 April

Ann uses an adjournment debate in the House to attack the closure of Tower and to highlight its effect on the economy of the Cynon Valley. In her speech, Ann says that Neil Clarke *"has debased, demeaned and diminished public life. As a public servant, there is only one last thing that in honour he should do. He should resign from public life and promise never to return."*

Ann also attacks the President of the Board of trade and his Minister for Energy, who *"have practiced a massive deception"* on the miners.

Dutch barn used to keep coal dry before delivery by rail to Aberthaw Power Station

8 February 1997

6.45 pm

Car park

21 February 1997

7.16 pm

Head lampman
30 January 1997
1.26 pm

Ready for work

30 January 1997

1.14 pm

Beginning of the afternoon shift

Dai Silcox, loading bay

28 August 1996

1.10 pm

Lamproom

Andrew Broome, faceman

28 August 1996

1.32 pm

Miners collecting their cap lamps

Mike, fitter

28 August 1996

1.40 pm

A fitter checking the progress of underground equipment

3 October 1996

12.02 pm

Pit head

Mel Rees, overman

3 October 1996

7.45 pm

Pit head gear

21 February 1997

8.10 pm

John Woods, overman

30 January 1997

2.06 pm

Pit bottom, Tower 4

John Lewis, hitcher

31 October 1996

12.42 pm

V38 coal face

21 November 1996

8.22 am

Fitters working on the Dosco LH 1300

21 November 1996

11.22 am

Malcolm on the man-rider conveyor belt coming from the coal face

21 November 1996

9.05 am

Martin O'Donnel, FSV driver. FSV's are special vehicles, used to transport materials underground

31 October 1996

10.00 am

The west lateral intake V39-gate junction (under construction)

21 November 1996

10.46 am

Paul Quinn on the V38 coal face

21 November 1996

8.50 am

Face workers eating their food on the V38 tail road

Noel Hale, Roger Moseley, Paul Evans and Dai Thompson

31 October 1996

9.20 am

West Bute pumps - repairing the pipe pumping column

Dai 'Magic' and ventilation officer, Geraint Hodder

21 November 1996

12.26 am

Repair work being carried out near the V39 gate junction

21 November 1996

11.00 am

Hugh Brown, linesman, on the coal face

31 October 1996

10.47 am

A miner working on the Dosco LH 1300

21 November 1996

10.48 am

Geoff Davies, surveyor, on the West Bute man rider

21 November 1996

12.36 am

Dai 'Budgie' Jones, Strata Bunker

21 November 1996

12.36 am

Colliery officials at the end of the afternoon shift

Mel Rees, overman

14 September 1996

7.36 pm

Danny John in the FSV garage underground

31 October 1996

11.00 am

Washery, C.P.P. coal preparation plant

15 February 1997

12.36 am

'Snowy', underground contractor

30 January 1997

2.10 pm

The end of a morning shift

Lyn Williams, overman

27 September 1996

2.14 pm

The end of a morning shift

Gary Davies 'Knuckles' and Martin O'Donnel

28 August 1996

2.03 pm

The end of the afternoon shift

Mike Smith 'Jockey'

14 September 1996

7.27 pm

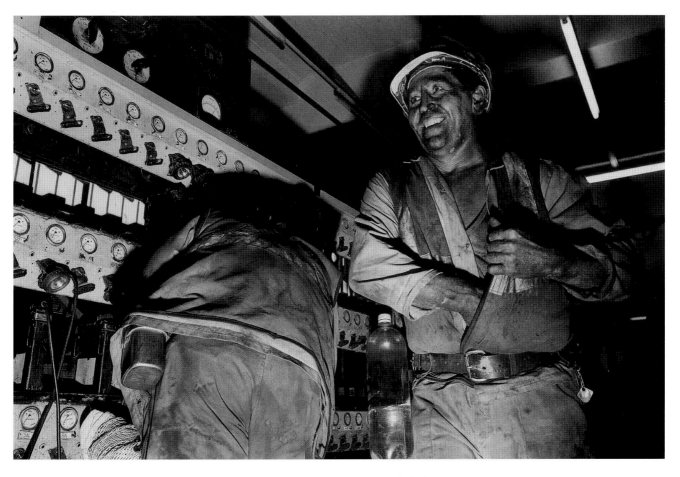

Miners putting their cap lamps on charge in the lamproom

3 October 1996

2.19 pm

There are two production shifts underground at Tower : maintenance is carried out over night

14 September 1996

7.31 pm

Lamproom

3 October 1996

2.25 pm

As the morning shift finishes, the afternoon shift are already underground

27 September 1996

2.18 pm

Bryn Sims rushing to get to the pit head baths

27 September 1996

2.02 pm

A miner talking to his mate in the fitting shop before going underground

3 October 1996

10.02 am

Miner walking towards the pit head baths

27 September 1996

2.21 pm

Offices

21 February 1997

9.03 pm

Martin O'Donnel

30 January 1997

2.18 pm

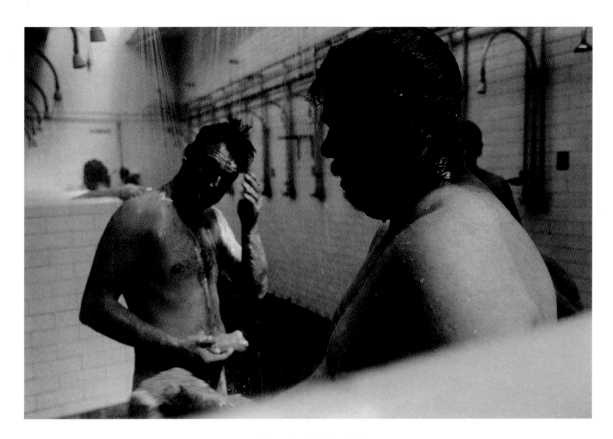

Showering after the shift

Neil Harper and Bob True, facemen

28 August 1996

2.05 pm

A miner moving from the dirty locker area into the showers

16 January 1997

2.35 pm

The pit head baths were introduced in many pits after nationalisation

16 January 1997

2.00 pm

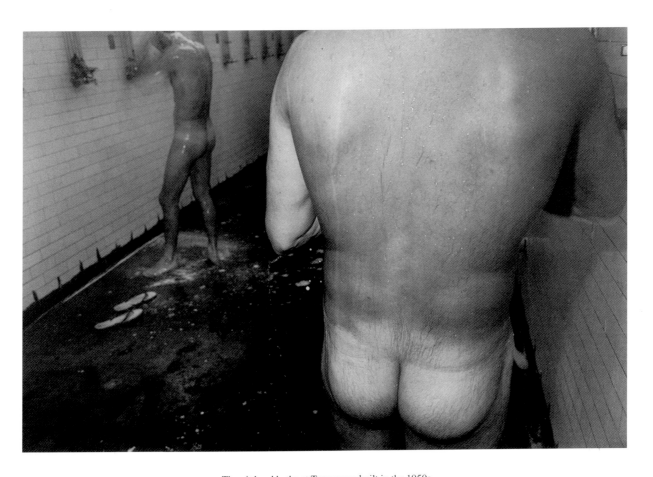

The pit head baths at Tower was built in the 1950s

16 January 1997

2.07 pm

Miners in the baths, discussing problems underground

Peter Griffiths and 'Bulldog'

16 January 1997

2.04 pm

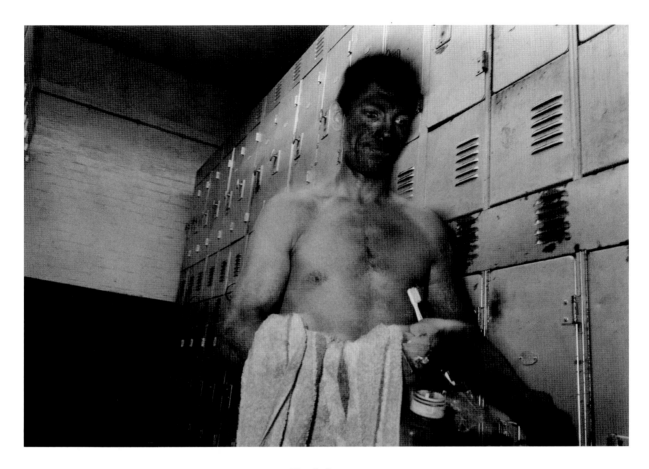

Dirty locker area

16 January 1997

2.31 pm

Completion of another shift

11 October 1996

2.41 pm

Offices

21 February 1997

9.41 pm

Washery

15 February 1997

8.33 pm

Wendyl Morgan, lampman

30 January 1997

2.00 pm

A coal merchant collecting coal ready to deliver to domestic customers in the Cynon Valley

7 October 1996

8.05 am

Rich seems of high quality Welsh anthracite is mined, and sold all over the world

7 October 1996

8.17 am

Jeff Williams, weigh bridge

19 September 1996

2.25 pm

A lorry being loaded with coal, ready for dispatch to British Steel, Port Talbot

7 October 1996

8.17 am

Driver in a road cleaning lorry at the washery

7 October 1996

11.59 am

Men working on the washery drainage system

Les Jones, surface worker and Gamon, who usually works as a faceman underground

31 January 1997

11.17 am

John Cummins looking at repair work on machinery in the washery plant

7 November 1996

10.14 am

Driver checking his lorry before coal is loaded onto it

7 November 1996

3.55 pm

Coal placed near the Dutch Barn, waiting to be transported by rail

10 October 1996

8.37 pm

Coal storage area

7 October 1996

9.29 am

Office cabins

21 February 1997

8.17 pm

30 January 1997

2.33 pm

Control room, monitoring underground conveyors and pit surface security

10 October 1996

9.03 am

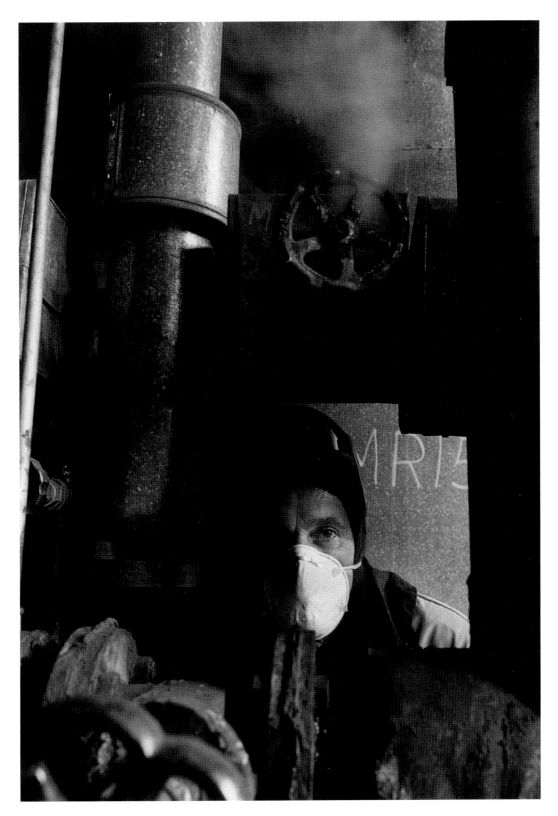

Mike Mahagan, boiler man

10 October 1996

10.50 am

The boiler being cleaned

10 October 1996

11.20 am

Repair work on underground machinery

7 November 1996

8.56 am

Tyrone O'Sullivan explaining the history of Tower to visitors

16 January 1997

10.21 am

Construction of the underground simulation unit which will be used for training

Glyn Roberts and Dai Thomas 'Magic'

10 October 1996

10.45 am

Repair work in the fitting shop

3 October 1996

9.59 am

Tower NUM Lodge Chairman, Glyn Roberts

16 January 1997

11.16 am

Miners in the pit canteen

19 September 1996

12.45 am

Young trainee, Glyn Roberts (junior) taking a break with Roger Moseley and Mike Fleet.

Mike and Roger usually work underground, although coal is sometimes not mined on Friday

24 January 1997

10.45 am

Mal, winding house operator

Mal used to work in Maerdy Colliery, Rhondda Fach, until he was forced to move after its closure

11 October 1996

8.47 am

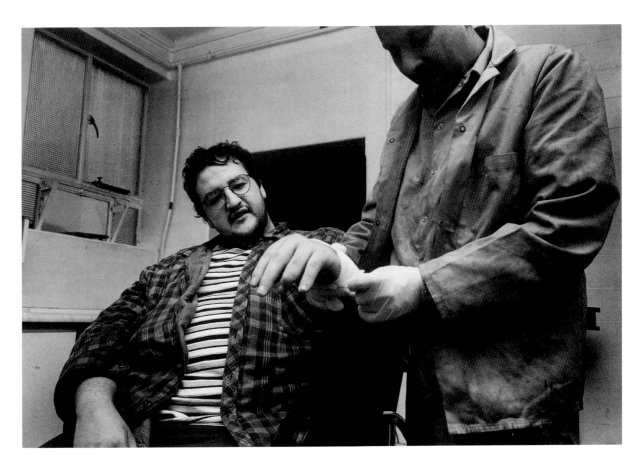

'Steve Williams 'Sqeaky' putting a bandage on Robert Williams in the medical centre

16 January 1997

8.36 am

Moving used supplies from underground through the drift to the surface

31 October 1996

11.32 am

Break time, fitting shop

3 October 1996

10.17 am

Fitting shop

3 October 1996

11 .23 am

Miners talking about the progression of the new coal face

Gary Cutlan and Clive Williams 'Fluff'

3 October 1996

11 .00 am

Burnt ashes from the boiler house being dumped

10 October 1996

11 .45 am

Pit canteen

Kevin Hewlett and Chris Jones

19 September 1996

12.37 am

Repair work on the road to the drift

Glyn Roberts (junior), Mike Fleet and Roger Moseley

31 October 1996

9.10 am

Washery

15 February 1997

10.03 pm

Lee Williams, trainee

30 January 1997

2.47 pm

Tower miners out on Friday night

17 October 1996

8.17 pm

Children at the Tower versus Rhigos rugby match

8 September 1996

3.15 pm

A retired miner at the Tower pub sports evening, Abercwmboi Rugby Club

Terry Kelly, Alan Dyton, Phil Thomas 'Phil the dog'

17 October 1996

10.28 pm

Tower children's Christmas party, Penywaun Club

7 December 1996

3.00 pm

A young girl watching a rugby match at Rhigos Rugby Club

8 September 1996

3.46 pm

Tower rugby team returning to the changing rooms at the open cast site after losing the match

Mark Jones 'Young bulldog'

8 September 1996

4.35 pm

An ex-Tower miner keeping fit in the weights room at the colliery

9 January 1997

9.32 am

Children's Christmas party

7 December 1996

4.12 pm

Tower miners enjoying themselves at an evening organised by the social committee at the colliery

17 October 1996

10.00 pm

Children dancing to the music at the Penywaun club

7 December 1996

4.23 pm

Miners use the gym on a regular basis to keep fit

Chris Earlan, plant maintenance officer

9 January 1997

10.15 am

Young boys in the freezing cold, near the coal tip

23 December 1996

4.05 pm

Tower darts match

Brian Griffiths and Martin Parsons

17 October 1996

8.59 pm

Hirwaun Junior School

5 December 1996

3.05 pm

Tony Jones is a committee member of his local football team in the village of Penrhiwceiber

1 March 1997

3.56pm

New companies are coming to the Cynon Valley employing mainly women

23 April 1997

11.17 am

View above Tower Colliery overlooking the Brecon Beacons

19 December 1996

11.55 am

Dai Thompson and Peter Griffiths 'Bulldog'

30 January 1997

3.00 pm

Mobile photographic studio erected in the lamproom using two studio lights and a canvas background.

Kim Howells, photographed at his home in Pontypridd. Kim was a pleasure to photograph, because he did not stage-manage the shoot. He gave me the freedom of making photographs in his kitchen; many would have moved the washing, that was hanging in the back ground, but Kim allowed me to create the image I wanted. With the daffodil and notes on the table in the foreground, and the Welsh dresser in the background, the composition creates a strong perspective within this environmental portrait.
Using a combination of flash and a long exposure, I decided to capture him in a different surrounding, not usually associated with a politician.

Whilst waiting for the cage to descend, ready to take us back to the pit surface, I made some photographs of Malcolm and Geoff. The pit bottom was lit with a series of fluorescent lights, so the exposure was shorter than other areas underground in the pit.

I went up to interview and photograph Tyrone and his wife on a misty Saturday morning in the middle of Winter. After photographing Tyrone inside his home, I decided to take some pictures of him in the playground opposite his house. He was very helpful and easy going, a pleasure to photograph.

The last photograph I made for this book was at the House of Commons. Ann Clwyd agreed for me to interview her and also make some photographs. There are strict photographic restrictions at the House of Commons. While I waited in the main lobby, I thought that I would be able to get some strong environmental portraits of Ann. But restrictions will only allow photographs to be made in limited areas.
Going in the House of Commons is an experience that I will never forget. Ann Clwyd and her research assistant were very helpful.

Mr Jones lived in the village of Hirwaun, situated a few miles from Tower Colliery. I wanted to find a miner who remembered the old days at Tower. After going to the local library, I eventually found Mr Jones. His memory was fantastic; he remembered every date, event and the names of all the men he worked with.
I photographed Mr Jones in his kitchen, using bounce flash off the wall behind me. Mr Jones had his electric fire switched on and I was so close to it making this photograph, my fleecy coat was starting to melt.

I met Tony Jones at the coal face in Tower Colliery; he was such a nice bloke. I asked him if I could interview him and his wife at their home. They live in Penrhiwceiber, in a terraced house overlooking a new industrial estate; the new factories were built on land which had been reclaimed from an old colliery site.
Tony and his wife are proud of their family and their home: I felt so welcome there. After having tea and biscuits, I photographed the couple in their living room, using bounce flash.
Tony's wife travels daily to Cardiff, down the valley to work, while he travels up to Tower at the head of the Cynon Valley.

32   Liz Manning has lived in Aberdare all her life. She runs a stall at Aberdare market and is the organiser of many community events in the town.
I came across Liz after watching her on a regional television documentary. This gave me the idea of using the television in the photograph with a picture of her on the screen. Her son was also at home on the evening I visited Liz, so I felt it appropriate to include him in the photograph. I used bounce flash as my main light source.

37   When the photographs for this book started to take shape, I decided to put the images in visual chapters. To start each series, within the set, I wanted to use a landscape image. I felt it would be interesting to make all the landscape photographs at night, in order to give a mysterious feel to the strong metal shapes that are associated with the mining industry.
This image was made, exposing the film for six minutes during which, I painted areas of the scene with multiple flash. It must have looked pretty weird for the passing motorists on the nearby road.

38   Perhaps photographers visiting Tower Colliery are more attracted to the pit head wheel than the car park.
Again choosing to make the picture at night, I used multiple flash and a long exposure. The cars show a sign of the times, as miners in the past walked to work.

39 & 40   The lampman, (39) photographed in the portable studio holding a check tag given to miners going underground. (40) Underground worker on his way to the cage.

41   One of the first images I captured for this book was a miner walking towards the lamproom to pick up his lamp and begin his shift underground. I waited, crouched on my knees to get a dramatic low angle. After waiting about ten minutes, I made this photograph. The miner walked through the narrow corridor, ignoring my camera as he turned into the lamproom.

42   I decided to make the photographs and place them in sections, choosing areas of which to record during each visit. As with the previous image, and the following picture, I wanted to capture the miners with clean faces, before their shift started.

43   The miners are so high-spirited and it is a pleasure to witness their friendliness and humour. It is difficult to take pictures sometimes, as I am laughing so much at their wit.
Photographing through the rows of lamp batteries and charger racks creates interesting graphic shapes. I was pleased with this photograph because the two miners, for a fraction of a second, moved into the perfect position and I pressed the shutter release.

44   The work tools that the underground fitter carries can make interesting images. The dirt and grime illustrate the nature of the miner's work.

46   Photographed at night, at the rear of the pit head wheel. I used multiple flash to paint the area with light, the shutter was left open for ten minutes.

47   A portrait of a miner after his shift underground. Photographed using a portable studio in the lamproom.

48   The environment underground is a man's domain. Unlike large coal mines in North

America, where around two percent of women work underground, coal mines in Wales, historically have never employed women to work underground. This photograph was taken using a wide aperture, in order for the viewer to focus on the 'MEN' sign. The banksman stands in the middle of the image, against the cage safety barrier on pit bottom.

49   After travelling on moving conveyor belts to shorten the journey underground, we arrived at the coal face, which is about five miles from pit bottom. Accompanied by Malcolm and Geoff, who are surveyors, I set up my camera on a tripod. Obviously conditions are hostile: it is dark, dirty and damp; not ideal conditions to make photographs in. Ordinary batteries are not allowed underground, as they could cause an explosion. So a flash gun and light meter were out of the question. The shutter on my camera works mechanically, and exposures were made, lasting from five seconds to two minutes. Some areas underground were extremely dark.

50   Some of the main roadways underground were lit by fluorescent lighting. Using my cap lamp and some spot lights, the exposures were quite short. I had to guess the exposure, and tell the men to stay still while they were painted with light.

51   Riding the conveyor belts underground is an experience I will never forget. You climb onto a platform and just drop down onto the moving conveyor and lie down on your front. To get off, you have to stand up and prepare to jump onto a platform. I've never been so nervous in all my life, but I didn't tell Malcolm and Geoff. They were used to travelling on these conveyors, so they carried my camera equipment and tripod.
The system of conveyor belts take the freshly cut coal from the coal face to the surface, for washing, grading and transit.

52   As we were walking through one of the dark roadways underground, a vehicle, known as a FSV came towards us. I heard the driver shout, Rog! I walked towards the driver and he shook hands with me. It was Martin, who I met a few weeks ago on the pit surface. The comradeship is unbelievable, Martin remembered my name.
I photographed him sat in the FSV using the lights on his vehicle and my cap lamp.

53   There are numerous road ways underground at Tower. Usually, you will come across maintenance crews working. It can be eerie underground, as the dim lit tunnels disappear into infinity.

54   The V38 coal face is long in distance, but low in height. It was hard carrying my camera equipment, trying to watch my footing and walking parallel to the coal face with restricted height room of between four and five feet.
When we got near the coal cutter, it was moving across the coal face, covering us with a water jet. Everything was wet and dirty, including my face. I set up the tripod in the wet, a few inches deep in black slurry and photographed the face workers. The light conditions for photographing was far from adequate, but the rays of light from the miners helmets created interesting beams.

55   The boys eating their food in the V38 tail road. My camera lens kept steaming up, as it was very warm in this part of the mine. Roger, second miner from the left, informed me when the lens needed cleaning. One of the boys gave me toilet tissue, kept under his helmet, which he had not used, so that I could clean the lens.

56   Trying to keep all the men still during a ten second exposure was impossible. When I told them to carry on working, so that I could get some movement though, they were more interested in posing for the camera. It was noisy, but I could hear them joking with each other. All the men at Tower Colliery were good humoured and friendly.

57   Some of the machinery underground needs to be assembled and repaired on site. Using my cap lamp and a few spot lights, it allowed me to produce the image using strong highlight and deep shadow. Instead of photographing the machine as a whole, which was large and complex, I decided to select the under-side of the machine, eliminating complexities and recording simplistic shapes against the miner at work.

58   In most of my images, I use a lot of blacks. Photographing underground is probably the most suitable for me to make images, as there is no shortage of black.

59   Using perspective as a means of scale in the long, seemingly never ending shafts can create interesting images.
I remember at this point, roughly four hours into my visit underground, the heavy steel toe-capped boots I borrowed, were rubbing the heels of my feet. The sweat was dripping from my face mixed with the coal dust and my camera was steaming up; it was pretty hot down there.

60   This photograph was made not far from pit bottom, on the way back from the coal face. Miners ride the West Bute man-rider at the end of their shift, as part of their journey back to pit bottom.

61   The miners underground were so helpful in making all these images. They did everything I asked of them. It is not easy to stay still for between ten seconds and two minutes, especially when you have a job to do. Nobody complained or refused to be photographed, and they still produced coal.

62   Back on the surface, the mine officials discuss problems underground.
Most of the miners have nicknames - 'Cardiff', 'Squeaky' and 'Pussy', to name a few.

63   This image was made in the FSV garage underground. It is an area in which mobile underground vehicles are taken to be repaired.

64   The washery is situated down the road from Tower Colliery. I gained permission to go onto the washery site on the weekend. During the day, it is quite busy, with vehicles moving around, and noisy machinery processing the coal. In the night, the site is quiet. As Tower is situated at the head of the Cynon Valley, it is susceptible to the cold winter winds blowing over from the Brecon Beacons and the strong driving rain; it was very cold and wet.
Using a long exposure and multiple flash to light the foreground, I walked around the area and set off my flash gun. Because the exposure was long, my body did not record on the film during the flash sequence.

65   A portrait taken in the lamproom using the portable studio.
All miners carry bottles of water underground for refreshment. This miner was carrying his empty bottle in his mouth, while he was putting his lamp back. So I asked if I could photograph him with his bottle in his mouth.

66   Most of the time I visited Tower Colliery, it was raining. If you are afraid of getting your camera wet or dirty, Tower is not the place to take photographs. Waiting for the miners to come up from underground to the surface, via the cage, can cause technical problems with the lens getting wet.

67   This picture was made using a slow shutter speed and flash. I moved the camera during the exposure to blur the background, while movement was created with the two miners walking past. The flash gun enabled me to gain detail in the foreground of the photograph.

68   Miners walking through the corridor from the cage in the background. Flash, this time was the main light source, but the bright cap lamp continued to record during a half second exposure.

69   After miners have finished their shift underground they race to the lamproom to put their cap lamps on charge, ready for the next day.
This photograph could easily be mistaken for an image from the 1950s, although this image of a miner is not a common sight anymore in the South Wales valleys.

70   Miners returning from underground, photographed in the evening, using flash and a long exposure.

71   Because the miners come into the lamproom quickly, as they want to get to the pit head baths, it is difficult to judge the ideal position to make the photographs. Telling the men to pose for a picture would not be the same as capturing them naturally.

72   One of my favourite images from the book is this one. Using the technique of movement and flash, you can never be absolutely sure of the result. By placing the flash more or less on the floor, it gave me a limited area in which the flash gun would light. So the second miner was only lit by daylight, while the man in the foreground was lit by a mixture of flash and daylight.

73   Another wet and misty day at Tower.

74   After having a nice strong cup of tea and a talk with the boys in the fitting shop rest room, discussing politics and rugby, I set about taking photographs of them: simplifying cluttered shapes is difficult. Using flash, not only as a light source, but as a creative extension of composition, can produce interesting, and sometimes abstract forms.

75   Miner returning from underground.

76   This image was made lit with flood lights, which light the road into the colliery.

77   Miner photographed in the portable studio set up in the lamproom.

78   The pit head baths always forms an interesting location to make photographs. I was told once that a photographer working for the Telegraph newspaper visited a pit in Yorkshire and when he tried to make photographs in the pit head baths, the miners threw soap at him. This has never happened to me at Tower, or any other colliery in the South Wales coalfield, when they were in operation.

79   A picture made, as a black-faced miner walks past the lockers in the foreground.

80   After coming into the baths from the cold outside, the hot water causes condensation and the camera lens to steam up.

81   Being a photographer can be embarrassing sometimes.

82   Anticipating the action and then finding the right angle and moment to make the image always fascinates me. This image contrasts the working process of the miner, from the dirt underground through to leaving the pit clean again. The miner is still in work clothing, dressed on the left, while the soap covered miner washes the grime away. The miner in the background dries himself ready to dress into his clean clothes.

83   The interest in this photograph, like many others in this series, is the juxtaposition of objects. The clean towel and tooth brush, carried by the dirty miner.

84   The facade to the entrance of the pit head baths tends to stand out from the regimented brick work structure. In nearly all the pits in South Wales, the baths were added, long after the original sinking of the pit.

85   A long exposure recording the main administration offices at the colliery.

86   An image recorded at the coal washery site using multiple flash and available light.

87   Portrait of the lamp attendant in the lamproom using the portable studio.

88   As part of my photographic documentation of Tower, I felt it important to show the finished product, 'coal'. I waited for the coal lorry to pull up and the coal merchant to fill the sacks of coal. Against a stormy sky, the silhouetted shape of a man was captured.

89   I walked up onto the gangway to photograph coal moving on the conveyor belt and dropping into a lorry below.

90   The coal that leaves the Tower washery is weighed at the weigh bridge. The men working at Tower are proud to be able to continue producing high quality coal in the Cynon Valley. They have proved by running their pit successfully, that there is a market for coal. Listening to them talk, was an educational experience. They all had a common belief, which is to fight for the right to work.

91   I thought the driver of this lorry was posing for me to make a photograph, but he was checking to see when his truck was full, as the coal was being loaded via a conveyor belt.

92   Perhaps the relationship between coal and cleanliness is a contradiction in terms. Tower's main aim is to produce coal, although every effort is made to keep the colliery site clean and tidy.

93   A new drainage system was being constructed near the washery. It was raining heavily and the water was rushing into a drainage canal. I managed to get some shelter under the temporary plastic covering and subsequently made this image.

94   The washery building is a large structure, dimly lit and full of heavy machinery. After walking up a few flights of metal stairs, I found this group of miners working on a piece of equipment. It was dark, and difficult to focus my lens.

95   Sometimes you see an image where the lighting and subject composition is strong, but just missing an extra dimension. As I looked through the camera view finder, the lorry driver left his cab and climbed up onto the back to see if it was empty. As he got to the top, he was silhouetted against the sky, making the perfect missing element to the photograph.

96   A consignment of coal which travelled down on conveyor belts from the coal face via the coal washery plant, ready to be moved by rail.

97   When there is heavy plant machinery moving coal onto lorries, it can be dangerous. An illuminating yellow coat and a safety helmet is essential to make sure the operators know that you are there.

98   The office spaces at Tower are more practicable than decorative, in comparison with modern electronics factories, which have designer furniture.

99   Miner photographed at the portable studio in the lamproom.

100   The control room not only covers the security of the pit on the surface, but monitors the coal production process underground. Any problems with the transport of coal from the face, can be monitored and the controller can alert mechanical and electrical engineers, in order to solve occurring problems quickly.
Making a photograph in this room was difficult, because it was visually not particularly interesting. I decided to use flash from low down, to give the image a surreal feeling, with the controller in the foreground.

101   This image of Mike was made using daylight from a window to the right hand side of the room. The boiler house was noisy and it was difficult to communicate over the monochromatic tones of the machinery.

102   Again using flash from a low angle, I wanted to catch the ashes of coal being taken from the boiler. To cool the ashes down, water was sprayed on them. With a mixture of water and heat, a screen of smoke filled the room. I had to wait until some of the smoke cleared before making this image.

103   Using and distorting scale can produce an interesting composition.

104   Tyrone's philosophy is to let as many people know about the success of Tower as he possibly can. His passion for Tower Colliery always comes across, and the numerous times that I talked to him, he taught me a lot about true values in life.

105   Miners making the footing for the new underground simulation for training apprentices and up-dating the skills of existing miners.

106   The shapes of cogs and wheels on the machinery can create a graphic surrounding, in which the subject automatically falls into place. The lads in the fitting shop were a great bunch.

107   Glyn is the Chairman of the National Union of Miners at Tower. He is also a member of the management committee.
Glyn is a real character and trying to photograph him without laughing is impossible. Eventually, he forgot about me taking photographs and concentrated on his union business.

108   The pit canteen is still a meeting place for the miners.

109   After taking photographs of men at work near the washery, I was invited in from the torrential rain for a hot cup of tea. Apart from the pit canteen, the miners on the surface have rest areas in the particular part of the pit in which they work. Glyn in the foreground, who is an apprentice at Tower, is the son of Glyn Roberts, the union chairman at Tower.

110   Mal used to work at Maerdy Colliery, over in the Rhondda Fach, until it closed. He was transferred to Tower, and he said it was the best thing that could have happened to him.

111   With the excellent safety record at Tower, the medical centre normally caters only for minor injuries. If there was a serious accident underground the medical centre would be the focal point of activity.

112   I used two photographs on this page, to juxtapose one image of work and one of rest.

113   During this photographic assignment, I became interested in looking at the clothing worn by the miners, as well as their faces. A lot of information can be gained by their overalls: how dirty they are and the accessories that hang from them.

114   Absenteeism of the workforce is extremely low, morale is high.

115   As Mike tips the ashes from the boiler house, I photograph him against the symbolic and historic pit head wheel, which for so many, is the lasting and graphic memory of the South Wales valleys.

116   The miners made life easy for me; they rarely played to the camera.

117   Sometimes, coal is mined four days a week, which allows the miners, who are usually underground, to work on the surface. This enables routine surface repair jobs to be carried out.

118   Area near the drift mine entrance. It was difficult to get to this position. Having to walk over a series of small slurry tips, proved to be a time consuming process. The slurry came up to my knees.

119   Miner photographed in the portable studio.

121   The day that the miners of Tower played rugby against the local village; I did not want strait sports shots of the rugby action.

122   The comradeship between existing and past miners at Tower is incredible. Nobody is forgotten, and everyone makes an effort to socialise, even outside work.

123   These boys, unlike their ancestors, may never grow up to work in the coal mining industry. Their future will probably take them away from the area.

124   A family day out as the Tower rugby team battle against Rhigos.

125   Tower boys walking to the make-shift changing rooms at the nearby open cast baths.

126 & 130   An ex-miner using the weights room at Tower Colliery (126). I waited a few weeks to catch somebody using the gym and then suddenly, there was an influx of keep fit fanatics.

127 & 129   The Penywaun Club was difficult to find. It was just off the main road, but I took a few wrong turnings. It was worth the trouble though.

128 & 132   Tower Colliery boys having a good time at Abercwmboi Rugby Club.

131   It was late afternoon and freezing cold, and I decided to walk around the coal tips. Two lads were walking their dog, one was wearing a balaclava, he looked sinister, although he was just keeping warm.

133   The young children will help towards creating future prosperity in the Cynon Valley. Hirwaun Junior School is an example of reaching high educational standards to help future generations in forming a positive future.

134   I went up to Penrhiwceiber to photograph Tony Jones, who works at Tower, and is on the committee of his local football team. His team lost this time, but the other team were placed near the top of their division.

135   Coal mining will never create thousands of jobs anymore. The new industrial base relates to clean high-tech industries which have been attracted to the Cynon Valley.

136   Visitors stop off for a picnic lunch, taking in the breath taking view of the Cynon Valley and the Brecon Beacons. The rural areas of the Brecon Beacons can clearly be compared against the industrial Cynon Valley, when scanning the panoramic view. Tower Colliery lies in the middle, which reminds us of the dramatic change, when the coal and iron industry transformed the rural valley landscape.

137   Miners photographed in the portable studio.

1960   Born in the South Wales valleys

Employment
1978-82   Industrial photographer at Lucas
1984-90   Freelance photographer
1986-present   Part time and visiting lecturer
1988-present   Lecturer and Head of Photography at Swansea College

Major Commissions, awards & bursaries
1985   Artist in Residence, Llanedeyrn High School, Cardiff
1986   Commissioned to photograph Artists in Residence around Wales
1986   Young Artists Award
1986   The Valleys Project, Ffotogallery, Cardiff
1988-91   The 1992 National Garden Festival
1992   The remains of the slate industry on the landscape in North Wales (Arts Council of Wales)
1993   The Brecon Beacons National Park
1994   Energy on the landscape. A series of images looking at the energy industry in Britain & Ireland (Arts Council of Wales)
1995   Welsh Books Council award
1996   Tower Colliery (Arts Council of Wales)
1997   Women living in the coal mining regions of West Virginia, Kentucky, Tennessee & Virginia, USA
1998   The Welsh in Pennsylvania, USA
1998   Short listed for the Independent on Sunday Photographic Awards

Books
1994   Hiraeth, a longing with the land
1994   Grazing Slateland
1995   The Black Valley the Grey Sky
1998   Owned by the Miners : Tower
1999   Merched Y Cymoedd & the American Dream
2000   Pennsylvania Welsh

Public Collections
Ffotogallery, Cardiff
The National Library of Wales
University of Tennessee, USA
Highlander Research Center, Tennessee, USA
The National Library of Scotland
Trinity College, Dublin

Web Sites
The National Library of Wales   http://www.llgc.org.uk/ardd/rtiley/rt001.html
Axis - Leeds Metropolitan University   http://www.lmu.ac.uk/ces/axis/